EARTH'S ALMANAC

To my family, in memory of Sally

Lucy Newlyn

EARTH'S ALMANAC

ENITHARMON PRESS

First published in 2015
by Enitharmon Press
10 Bury Place
London WC1A 2JL

www.enitharmon.co.uk

Distributed in the UK by
Central Books
99 Wallis Road
London E9 5LN

Distributed in the USA and Canada
by Independent Publishers Group
814 North Franklin Street
Chicago, IL 60610
USA
www.ipgbooks.com

Text © Lucy Newlyn 2015

ISBN: 978-1-910392-10-2

Enitharmon Press gratefully acknowledges the financial support of
Arts Council England, through Grants for the Arts.

Individuals contribute to sustain the Press through the
Enitharmon Friends Scheme. We are deeply grateful to all Friends,
particularly our Patrons: Colin Beer, Sean O'Connor and those
who wished to remain anonymous.

British Library Cataloguing-in-Publication Data.
A catalogue record for this book is available
from the British Library.

Designed in Albertina by Libanus Press
and printed in England by
Short Run Press

CONTENTS

If it were a life	9
Leaves	10
Thaw	11
Snapshots	12
February	13
Three winters ago	14
Starry tree	15
Your lost poem	16
My pear tree	17
March 20th	18
Telling time	19
Meanwhile	20
The intruder	21
As, so	22
Inscription	23
Stray	24
Missing	26
Not ours	27
Cherry tree	29
French windows	30
From the loft	32
Long vacation	34
It came in July	35
A rebellion	36

A Cumbrian summer

I	Derwentwater	38
II	Screen-prints	40
III	Tracks	41
IV	The swallows	44
V	A midsummer night	45
VI	Found	46
VII	Total eclipse	47

Genius loci	48

Auguries from abroad

I	A Romantic pilgrimage	49
II	Pompeii	50
III	Jiuzhaigou	51

Sally	53
Two songs in August	54
Autumn	55
Leave-taking	56
Conkers	57
The hedge	58
Raking leaves	59
The end	60
Sally's photo	61
Yew	62

The Year's Midnight

I	Hope in November	65
II	Hourglass	66
III	Enlive	67
IV	Her window	68
V	December	69
VI	Then	70
VII	(And then again)	71
VIII	Morning	72
IX	Membrane	73
X	Untitled	74
XI	Taking stock	75
XII	The house	76
XIII	Her shoes	77
XIV	Keepsakes	79
XV	Anniversary	80
XVI	Reminders	81
XVII	About time	82

Memory's Music

Land's End	85
Name-placing	86
Choughs	87
Portloe: looking Westward	88
Hiraeth	89
Term-time	90
Second homes	91
Veryan Green	92
The road to Veryan	93
Pendower	96

Wracks

I	Rock-pools at Carne	98
II	Mermaiden weeds	100
III	Unsolved riddle	101
IV	Fetched up	102
V	Remedies	103
VI	Toothed Wrack	104
VII	Bladder Wrack	104
VIII	Oar-weed, or Tangle	105
IX	Sea-oak	105
X	Old names	106
XI	Re-cycled	106

Harvest	107
High tide in October	109
Walter Langley's *The Breadwinners*	111
Wreck	113
Invisible	114
Remembering the eclipse	115
A winter walk	118
Acknowledgements	120

If it were a life,
unfolding like a year,
it would begin and end with snow.
If I could tell it leaf by leaf, then you'd be there,
catching the morning light, the way our cherry tree
was there – in the unnoticed middle ground,
with the snowdrops in January, or the feathery grass in summer,
giving the long snaking path something to travel round.
You were always outside the frame.
I knew you so well I no longer saw you.
When they came,
with their ropes and axes, and a truck
to cart away the pieces,
did I watch
and
listen,
to keep
your
shape
more
clear?
I carry it in my mind, like a poem the words
keep changing – each day, each month, each year.

LEAVES

January, and I am reaching out for leaves,
or memories of leaves, like things stowed away
in attics, or dark cupboards under eaves.

Whose trees are these, known only
by feeling round their edges?
Whose hands, whose leaves?

THAW

Suppose it were like this always:
the city time-locked, white-hooded;
the streets deserted,
the houses gone all quiet, the survivors
coming towards us in the final scene –
humbled and thankful, exchanging stories,
saved for the new beginning.
Suppose it could happen like this
all over again, and still mean the same,
as if someone were gently shaking
a transparent ball,
and making the snowflakes fall . . .

*

Edge by gradual edge, shapes
re-surface, like rocks and driftwood
above an ebbing tide.
Smooth undetermined contours
loosen and shrink, textured patches
spread and darken.

*

Packed solid, huge snowmen
kept watch for days like alien sentries,
the last to melt. Now they are
broken cromlechs,
cairns islanded by greenness,
soft illegible milestones.

SNAPSHOTS

A man on a crumpled rug alongside his baby
sits tending a small child in a white dress
with smocking. She walks carefully,
like a nun or a bride, looking downwards
and forwards. These are not her first steps:
she smiles quietly to herself as she moves
toward the camera, and out of the frame.

Forty years away, a woman stands looking
through an open door, to where an old man sits
beside his daughter. She is lying in bed, wearing
a white linen nightdress, and has turned
to face him. They are waiting. He holds
her hands, her eyes, her heart, steadily in his.
Firstborn: on this retina she doesn't fade.

FEBRUARY

Houses steeled, with their blinds tight shut,
the days short, birds mute, the streetlamps lit.

Earth like flint, sky stretched taut,
shrubs stripped bare, with their roots hard-bit.

Hedges holding back from the street,
clenched as a fist and dark as night.

Trees driven deep in their sockets, stalky-stiff
with their sap sunk, and their ribbed bark thick.

Birds stock still, their spirits pent,
light neaped, the earth spent.

THREE WINTERS AGO

Three winters ago
from my kitchen window
I saw him –
sudden against snow.

Eyes alert, head tilted,
crest a curlicue of red,
he stabbed about
on the back lawn, distracted,

then worked up
the pear tree, tap-tap-
tapping as he went:
a jerky vertical.

I've watched out for him
many times since then –
my perpendicular guest,
my emerald ice cragger –

and now the new year
has come round again,
I hope to see him
as I saw him when

he came three years ago,
sudden against snow –
his beak in tune with tree-time:
pulse of the tree.

STARRY TREE

Magnolia stellata, starry tree,
tree in my window-frame
like a silk-screen from Japan –
white stars on a smooth black stem.

Magnolia stellata, lovely tree,
tree of the magical name:
the only tree in flower
when the snowdrops came.

Magnolia stellata, early tree,
tree early enough for one
who died before the crocuses
had been and gone.

Magnolia stellata, only tree
who remembers
(as the cold earth
remembers) one unborn.

Magnolia stellata,
tree of the magical name,
tree in my window-frame:
only early lovely starry tree.

YOUR LOST POEM

No comparison
but I'm drawn to making one
with the black sack

I witnessed on a screen:
nothing inside it, not a single track
or trace to say that life had ever been.

Nothing can stop you knowing
and of course you know
it must have come adrift by now

scattered abroad
to the four winds and blown
about like thistledown.

Watch closely though
in a cleft between two rocks, a hollow,
your new poem in embryo.

MY PEAR TREE

has roots deep as itself
but the half of it I see

stands only a few yards away
sturdy as a citadel.

Its knobbly wind-bent branches
will swell and foam white in May.

In autumn it will drop
huge scarred pears like burdens.

I check it hourly, like a sun dial.
The years turn in its shadow.

It's my lodestone,
spirit level.

I return to it each evening
and come down to it each day.

MARCH 20TH

If I kept a diary for every day,
what would this one say?
Suddenly and all at once it came,
in never-ending blue and softest green.
Overnight the plum tree turned white
and the pear-tree buds began their slow unfurling.
All along the street the air was sweet
with new mown grass – the year's first mowing.

TELLING TIME

Today, as the clocks go forward – one time
overlaying the other like a transparency –
I hold still for an hour, hesitating, in between.

How clearly everything composes itself
for a threshold scene: the garden coming into leaf,
daffodils shining on the lawn, the family
grouped under the pear-tree, turning this way.

Who is the child moving into the shade
and out of the picture? Her face keeps changing.
Always I'm watching just as she's going.
Time shuffles memories like a sheaf of leaves.

MEANWHILE

*A failure of attention,
you might call it – the mind
elsewhere, preoccupied.*

Perhaps it would be easier
to fast-forward and watch
the whole thing in reverse,

like scar tissue disintegrating
layer by layer
down to an open wound –

> the tree losing its girth,
> the hedge dwindling
> to a puny row of saplings,
>
> the family moving back
> through all the strange
> unfocused years,
>
> the girl re-emerging as she was
> before the photos
> and the bed-time stories stopped

than to track the narrative
through these thickening threads
as they multiply

and mesh together,
shutting so much from view.

THE INTRUDER

A cry brought me running.

I stood on the doorstep
(nipped, crisp-frosted)
watching.

The mist moved slowly, like a secret, along the lawn,
among the houses,
haunting the still trees.

There were no footprints.

Only a lean, low-bellied hunger
lingering on the air like a scent

and eyes

searching the darkness
as I closed the garden gate.

AS, SO

As the leaded veins
in a tall, stained-glass window
portion the sunlight,

so the sunk threads in
a shiny leaf, turned over,
lattice its fine grain.

INSCRIPTION

In broken patches
through the yew's branches
a Norman church.

Light catching the tower's corbels,
an empty porch.

On the lawn
a coverlet of crocuses,
an iris touching a gravestone,
books on a seat in the sun.

Under the yew
a mat of cyclamen,
blackbirds pecking the earth.

On the path
a silent signature of shadow,
lichen blurring an epitaph.

STRAY

It is sweet to enter that peacefullest and homeliest of churchyards, St Peter's in the East, overlooked by St Edmund Hall and Queen's College and the old city wall. There is a peace which only the thrush and blackbird break, and even their singing is at length merely the most easily distinguishable part of the great melody of the place. Most of the graves are so old or so forgotten that it is easy – and in Spring it is difficult not – to perceive a kind of dim reviving life among the stones, where, as in some old, quiet books, the names live again a purged and untroubled existence.

(Edward Thomas, *Oxford*: 1903)

Rain on mottled graves
and among long soft
fingers of yew. Rain
bending grasses, dark-
ening stones, pocking
grainy lichened tombs.

Often he'd wander in
alone – conjuring
the shades of Aubrey,
Browne and Hearne –
his Welsh soul probing
deep into English soil.

Along the wall
the ivy-leaved toadflax
hangs its delicate bells.
Fern fronds, heavy
with rain weight, lie
bowed down low.

On the path, hurrying
the other way, a young man
his age: head bent,
hand raised, listening
to his cell-phone, like
a traveller from afar.

High on the air waves,
signals weave and dance.
A lone blackbird flicks
between gables – quick
and random as the stray shell
that buried him in France.

MISSING
in memory of Susan Hurley

We'd sometimes wander round here
in the afternoons. She liked imagining
us a stone's throw from All Souls,

and knowing that only the wall
divided us from New. She half-wanted
the place to be grander, but saw

how beautifully its scale would do.
She loved the way light fell
on the church – deep shadow

slanting across the lawn, long grass
feathering the gravestones,
yellow crocuses nudging through.

She suggested foxgloves for the corner,
and insisted on geraniums for the border –
they must be 'Johnson's Blue'.

In her mind's eye she could follow
the Étoile d'Hollande, from bare-rooted plant
to lovely sprawling rambler.

*

With the gravestones uprooted,
the long grass mown, the wall cleared
of roses, the compost-heap gone,

a smart new path laid through
the weeded lawn, and shrubs planted
where the foxgloves and the ferns once grew –

could I really still come round here
expecting to find her?

NOT OURS
in memory of Graham Midgley

What earthly use were they to us, or we
to them? Hidden under the bric-a-brac,
scrap metal, disused deck chairs,

broken flowerpots, discarded bicycles –
ten years' worth of family detritus
not ours – we found them:

two sandstone lintels, hard-edged
but soft-grained and malleable
beneath a mason's or a sculptor's chisel.

'Yours for the asking.' And so he came
one day, with a big car and a golden labrador
who kept barking and chasing the children.

His laughter boomed, filling the garden
and spilling over into gardens not ours
as he loaded them in and carted them away.

Thrift for the thrifty, shape to a shaper's eye
he carved them. One a fertility symbol,
Bacchus-Priapus, stone-god phallus

under tendrilling vine, he gave to the Hall.
The other, sad featured anchorite,
thin and tall like a Modigliani,

with formal genitals and hands
like flowers, he returned to us –
seeing, he said, as it was ours.

Twinned lintels, paired portals,
facets of his nature graven in stone:
Lord of Misrule, ungovernable laughter,

and scholar quiet, cerebral – changing,
interchanging, in company and alone,
during his life and after.

From something bequeathed, unbidden,
something given to give. Mantles:
ours and not ours to give and be given again.

CHERRY TREE

If I could tell you
how the listening branches hung
deep and rich with their own dark shining
heavy with the weight of red
there'd be no need of elegies.

None of this speaks of her
none of it signifies
except through
premonitions, absences.

Already in May
white candles were lighted
in horse-chestnut trees.

FRENCH WINDOWS

It all followed as a matter of course
after the side of the house
was opened up, no one noticing at first

the train of consequences
which slipped one after the other
through French windows latticing the garden.

*

Silt of sunshine, tree dapple, sky's clarities
in glass, and the painting of walls
in various shades of sage, leaf, grass, apple.

A lifted carpet; the laying bare
and smoothing-down of a wooden floor.
A rug paved in warm earth colours.

The slow creeping over mantels and tables
of house plants. Shiver of leaf-shadow
and leaf shape, each side of windows.

*

Days lengthening, and the house hinged
on one side like a doll's, wide open
to the summer's murmurings:

laughter, to and fro of children;
smells of cooking along the breathing edges
of gardens. Tables and chairs spreading

from room to patio. Twist and flutter of birds
in a mirror, the tiny white thread of a plane
crossing the lacquered surface of the piano.

*

All day long, time's seepage between
floorboards. Knots darkening in the wood grain
like eyes. Cracks furring over with leaf spore,

lichen; butterflies folding on cushions,
the garden settling itself quietly into the room,
bringing the sky with it, and all its flitting,

velvety companions. At dusk the soft flap
of moths on light shades, or high up
in corners the webbed skin wings of bats.

*

And all this happening slowly,
as a matter of course, with no one noticing,
till one night coming down

to find the room a garden,
with the trees hushed, and the owls
hooting, and the windows still open.

FROM THE LOFT

Up here, where gardens flatten,
lose themselves
in composite blots of green,
and fences are pencilled markers
in a marbled pattern,
sky lifts and vanishes
in a weightless dream of blue –
a blue so light
that, dazed and halted
by transparency of height,
my vision drops
like a heavy plumb-line,
finding its own level
below the houses.

Steadied now, held safe
among cool laterals,
I'm hammocked
and rocked – threaded
sideways on quickening
stems of sound that rise
like thermals over tops
of trees, then drift as grainy
substances to the ground,
sifted through thickening
canopies of muffled leaves.

Tentatively, now,
I'm touching earth,
feeling under fences warm
with weeds, stirring
among blind creatures
moving back and forth

with nutrients and minerals,
through moist capillaries.
And slowly now,
provisionally,
I'm in the earth,
and under the porous earth
is carried a dream of blue,
and earth is being
carried.

LONG VACATION

The studio walls are trailed with writing,
in trembling spidery threads
parting, bending, touching, uniting

like luminous underwater weeds,
that slowly sway from left to right,
or hieroglyphs an unseen translator reads.

Above, through an open skylight,
patterns twist and fall
from an immense blue height

on tilted easel, mirror, table, wall.
Cloud shadow, wing flap, leaf motion
swarm in jars and phials, all

their fluctuation distilled into a potion
and veiled in thin green glass,
like micro-organisms in a gelid ocean.

Silence deepens as the days pass.

IT CAME IN JULY

It came in July, creeping sickening,
saddening – a deadly fear.

On a bench, in the glaring sun:
emptied garden, sister and dear sister,

her face pale with panic – or was it pain?
I asked her a question she couldn't answer.

Then, with a look I'd seen before,
five years before, almost to the day,

she left us, 'for a while' she said,
and went indoors, and stayed away.

Replica, spooky double,
first in a sequence of ghastly pairs,

your mouth set in silence, your head
framed in the doorway, your shadow

moving slowly upstairs: speak to me.
It is not too late. There is no never.

A REBELLION
in memory of JFW

He admired the long, low lines,
the rectangular, end-stopped blocks
running exactly parallel with the spaces

and broken only in the middle, with nothing
to interrupt the eye's steady passage
from opening to opening.

It was all urbanity and cool abstraction –
a Scandinavian utopia of vast skies,
clear vanishing-points, clean edges.

But none of this satisfied.

Was it mischief, or simply a longing
that made him plant seeds
in-between,

so that, over the years,
the roots worked their way
under?

As the rectangles loosened,
they lost their neat alignments,
and a softness came

in waves
and climbing, arching green.

Self-seeding, proliferating,
a thicket of unruly buddleias
sported their plumes near his window –

attracting, in August,
peacocks, red admirals, tortoiseshells,
fritillaries, and (once in a while)

a small white.

A CUMBRIAN SUMMER

I DERWENTWATER

A sudden twist of the wrist
sets the stones spinning
      like a question.
Blencathra's shoulders shiver as they skip
and dimple, spreading
        tiny   answers,
           fine   as   rain.

*

The eye can't focus,
shifting uneasily among
    motions,   agitations.

Murky grey-green water is cutting up rough:
massing ripples to challenge canoes
and baffle my dancing stones.

A spinning dinghy
      swings Cat Bells
round in its sling.

*

The white-sailed yacht
      tacks across Skiddaw's mighty shadow
like a fell-runner
      zig-zagging
down a path.

Dapper dragon-flies hold to the gorse.

*

As the wind slackens, the surface
flattens like a smooth sheet.

Mists fold away into themselves,
and bare-backed mountains

sink in reflections.

II SCREEN-PRINTS

Larches are ladies
in pale green, stepping lightly
along the lake-side.

Fastidiously
they lift their long skirts clear
of lapping water.

*

Tall pines lining
the lake's far edges are a child's
fold-and-cut festoon

of paper Christmas trees:
green hands holding green hands
round a blue lagoon.

*

Clouds contemplate only
themselves in a wide, bare,
superficial mirror.

Vain creatures: see how
they turn this way, that way,
for the most flattering slant.

*

Each of the branches
on the elegant larches
ends in a sloping down-stroke

with an upward flick:
signatures in green hand-writing
on a smooth blue lake.

III TRACKS

The lake is risen high, over
mossy stones and emerald grass.

Minnows dance where watery
celandines shine like fallen stars.

*

A small girl paddles the promontory,
trawling the water.

Her eyes scoop deeper than her yellow net,
under flickering silver.

*

She searches the pool, hearing
its steady ruminative conversation:

earlier than babble broken
in translation.

*

That skating insect's tiny pulsing
movement is a mind learning how to think.

It holds still for a moment, poised
over its own propulsion.

*

Beached in the shallows,
a rowing-boat rocks on the pebbles:

slup-slup under the creaking hull,
and long wooden oars chafe in their cradles.

*

Shape-shadows drift on the fells,
as shadow-shapes shift underwater.

Each side of the membrane,
a silent movie is playing both ways.

*

You can almost catch the drift
of an aeroplane by its long, spindly, trailing thread,

but scatter-tracks under water
are touch-less braille.

*

Nothing stays still on a lake. But tarns
on high fells hold deepest things down,

fermenting dull brackish
concentrates in peaty black stills.

*

Trails on the island criss-cross
and circle, open to question.

Gorse stiffens, prickly. Something
feral and restive stirs in the bracken.

*

Pocked and blistered silver cases
sheathe the lanky trunks of birches

but the tall, bark-stripped pine
is a skeleton: sudden and jagged.

*

Deeper in: needled ground – small, closed
pine cones in fallen thousands.

Fern-fronds under latticed beech-trees,
heavy with fallen rain.

    *

This noble ruin of a tree has
crumbled down to a single storey.

Woodlice scurry along secret
passages, hunting the hidden plot.

    *

Dusk on the island, and rooks behind us,
calling. Our boat leaves no tracks.

Only the low dissolving wash,
and long oars clunking in rowlocks.

IV THE SWALLOWS

'The swallows come to the sitting room window as if wishing to build but I am afraid they will not have courage for it, but I believe they will build at my room window. They twitter & make a bustle a little cheerful song hanging against the panes of glass, with their soft white bellies close to the glass & their forked fish-like tails. They swim round and round and again they come.'
         (Dorothy Wordsworth, *Grasmere Journal*, 16 June 1802)

What if they nested here, so close
we could almost touch,
and sense each other listening?

She settles, but they circle again
and again, the rushing
                    bubble of song
submerged by flap and wash of wings.

Magnified, they hang, bellies
pressed against the pane,
fins waving, bills silently opening.

Their eyes are aeons deep and away,
but looking in.
                    She's absorbed,
suspended in air, glass, water.

Something is stirring inside,
and they keep bumping, bumping
their soft white bellies up against my skin.

V A MIDSUMMER NIGHT

The wind came in the night
over Silver How, and stole my dream
like an egg from the nest,

flung the nest from the branch,
ripped the branch from the tree,
and tore the leaves away.

She's wide awake now,
guarding the tree
from stealthy, tiptoeing day.

VI FOUND

For too long the sky has bullied
the hills into submission.

Hindscarth, Dale Head, Robinson
lie sunk under a sodden weight of cloud,

their dark backs bowed and hidden.
Now, in sudden folds that heave

and shudder, chop and start,
the sullen waves are driven

across a lake recalcitrant
and leaden

as the rough, black, heart-shaped stone
she lugged home unbidden.

VII   TOTAL ECLIPSE

'It will come about in that day, that I will make the sun go down at noon and make the earth dark in broad daylight.' (Amos 8:9)

As the time approached, we wondered
if we'd see it differently –
she in Moseley, me in Manesty.

*

Through the long, tense, city summer
her calendar's empty windows
were highlighted with indelible stars.
Now, she was through with prognostications.

'In the clear!' Her voice sang down the line
with the joy of it, hills rang with it, lakes shone with it,
Castle Crag took up the sound.
All around, far and near, in the clear.

*

Punctually, I stood in the doorway
with a perfect view of the emerald valley
under its great dome of sky.

As the rooks flew creaking into the woods
I watched the shadow moving
slowly, exactly, across the sun.

Then the air darkened like an augury,
and earth grew chill.
August, die she must, season of treachery.

GENIUS LOCI

She's there again – bending, straightening,
bending, straightening – every so often
standing still, to get the measure of things,
take her bearings.
                    Is it some kind of witchery,
a trick of light, or this view of her the whole length
of the garden, that ghosts her into another time –
as if the houses behind had been folded up
and stowed away, like scenery?

She's there still – turning towards me, as if
to offer me something.

Runner beans perhaps, or a handful of sharp
gooseberries, wet from last night's rain.

AUGURIES FROM ABROAD

I A ROMANTIC PILGRIMAGE

We'd seen the Colosseum, the Vatican,
the Campo de Fiori. Now, on the third day,
it was the *Piazza di Spagna*.
(At home, tomatoes ripened on the vine
unpicked. Ground elder ramped in the border.
Bindweed trailed and clambered through spires
of buddleia, white trumpets blaring.
But this was Rome: *Sic transit gloria mundi*.)

Here Keats spat his last blood, cooped
in a dark airless chamber – listening
to cries of vendors on the Spanish steps,
or carriages turning in the dusty square.
We stood in awkward silence by his bed,
numbed by the absence coldly written there.
Reverent as pilgrims, or mourners paying
our respects, we shuffled out, clutching a cache
of postcards and souvenirs. I added my name
to the book of *'ubi sunts'* in useless tears.

Later, at the Protestant Cemetery,
we found his gravestone among trees.
(Space, paths, elegant cypresses; sun
beating on dry grass in early afternoon's
hot siesta stillness – the photos
slightly different from my memories.)
Light dances, now, among leaf-shadows
in our garden; flickers on *Here lies
One whose Name was writ in Water;*
picks out 'Bitterness of his heart . . .
Malicious Power of his enemies.'

II   POMPEII

He shelters inside, where
rain won't wear him down,
or human touch disturb him.

You'd almost think
the wall was still there
supporting him from behind,

he sits so firmly on his haunches –
back braced, feet planted
squarely on the ground.

If it weren't for the tensed neck
and shoulders, the head
bowed into upraised hands,

the doubled-up, nearly foetal
position, you'd assume he was
simply waiting, sunk in thought.

How endless his exposure,
naked and frail, to the absent
unimaginable scale of disaster.

Is he watching, or hiding?

His face is nearly covered
by his outspread fingers,
but not so that they shield his eyes.

III   JIUZHAIGOU

In China, one of the many
symbols for longevity is a crane.

There are no cranes wading
the lakes at Jiuzhaigou

where tens of thousands
of people come each day

to photograph water
clearer than any blue.

Nothing stirs on the side
of Yellow Dragon mountain.

No bats fly out of the tall woods,
darker than any silence.

The narrow path circles Swan Lake
without ever touching the water.

You must keep to the path,
directing your gaze

to the smooth azure, where no
goldfish or minnows swim.

At the bottom of Panda Lake,
skeletons of fallen pines

in their hundreds
lie sunk and still.

On a stone near the water's edge,
hope settles,

folds her delicate wings,
and is caught on film.

SALLY

Why, when I picture her,
is she so often turning towards me
under a tree, moving along a path,
or passing through a doorway?
And why, more often than not,
is it early evening?

Pausing under tall trees
in Headingley, she opens the front gate:
serious, short-haired, spectacled,
her school uniform worn proudly
as she walks toward the house,
through the rose-trellised archway.

In Headington, after much talk,
she's going inside to catch the tail-end
of Wimbledon. The boys have been lobbing
cherries at roof-tops all afternoon.
Looking back over her shoulder,
she smiles as she beckons me in.

Standing in the long thin garden
at Moseley, she's been searching
for something in the border.
It's summer; the barbecue's over.
We've cleared the chairs away,
and the kitchen door's ajar. I'm calling.

So much time has passed –
uncounted, silently – it would be hard
to tell 'before' from 'after'.
I can't hear what she's saying,
but her face is clearer than in the photos
I have of her, now hidden away.

TWO SONGS IN AUGUST

I
All day in the big lopsided cherry tree
the breeze has been whispering, whispering,
what is it you miss, what is it you are missing?

While the still, steady, warm croo-crooing
of stock doves high on Headington roof-tops
ponders an answer, refrains from answering.

II
The trees have spilled their summer on the lawn.
Apples lie wind-fallen, among dry leaves blown,
and heavy brambles lay their long arms down.

How have the hours flown, where have they gone?
So many promises like seeds not sown,
and only autumn left, to do or leave undone.

AUTUMN

This morning, I've watched mist slowly lifting
from houses, wind shifting among trees,
the first rays of sunshine touching three tall windows,
the gable of All Saints standing clear
and clearer against the sky, a stiff crane swinging
its arm round slowly over rooftops,
and – almost out of sight beyond the houses –
the blue-grey smudge of Shotover, shaping
into a woody hill.

It's all mapped out below me, this little slip
of land, once a market garden. Fences now portion
the orchard into separate plots, but from up here
among the chimneypots and aerials,
property lines are softened or erased
by untidy apple trees, the sprawl and scatter
of laden branches.

It's midday now. The edges of things
are visible, and where the edges end.
A bird flies toward its shadow on the brick-face
of the church. A silver plane slowly crosses
the sky. The prop for a washing-line sways
to and fro in the wind. Along Barrington Close,
the houses are open to view, and the man opposite
stands, as he often does, at his window.
I am now, and here. Knowing that the clarity
of things is enough, and would be
even if I were not among them, watching also.

LEAVE-TAKING

Branches ripple
under the wind's caress
in their skimpy autumn dress,

as though their one thought
were nakedness, and a quick
wintry consummation.

Their loveliness is too light,
too eager – like a child
walking gladly for the first time

to school alone,
without so much as a wave,
or a backward look towards home.

But here *you* are: stepping
carefully down the stairs,
in your beautiful blue dress

and high-heeled shoes,
with your long hair smooth
and combed – pausing

as you enter your fourteenth year,
to leave me
wordless, standing there.

CONKERS

Peeled, their padded rinds
discarded like old jackets,
they shine smooth and clean

as ocean-polished shells,
perfect as castings
loosened from their moulds,

entire unto themselves
as fresh-baked loaves, or podded
peas, or just-laid eggs, or berries.

You turn them over like a familiar
tune or a remembered line,
stilled by their touch and gleam.

Cool and hard they lie,
each one ringed concentrically
like the cross-section of a tree

in fold on fold of marbled gold-
sienna-chestnut-red-mahogany,
their dark sheen luminous

and naked as an eye.

THE HEDGE

We let it grow blind as a Cornish lane
sunk deep between hawthorn hedgerows,

ourselves the only things moving
behind eyes lidded and sewn.

Butchering it lowered the skyline,
anchored the street in tarmac.

Newly shorn, its punished sticks
are a stiff black jagged fretwork

the bright and sudden world
sees through. Light whelms, colours

skitter in jigsaw patches, traffic
is brazen-bodied with sound.

Houses opposite reach down a storey,
finding their own weight on the ground.

And now, in mid-September,
intrepid sproutings bring

a silvery, grey-green-grainy,
clove scented, unlooked for spring.

RAKING LEAVES

All week the wind has been stripping the trees,
and today the lawn is a sea of apples and leaves.

He's marooned. He turns in a circle, reaching
and hauling. His long rake is the net he's trawling.

He stands on his island, bending and scooping
the golden apples, landed among the cold wet leaves.

He sorts the leaves and apples all morning, working
from island to island, making the garden clean.

The lawn turns from brown to green. His catch
of apples is shining in piles under pristine trees.

THE END

As fallen leaves are cleared
and damaged fruit discarded

as things unfinished are laid to rest
alongside things accomplished

as bonfires burn
and sacrificial guys are lighted

it comes. Not suddenly
like a clock striking in the night

but steadily
beat after beat

like a foetus quickening
or a bird in flight –

the inexorable culmination
before breaking of waters

and rupture
in blank impartial light.

SALLY'S PHOTO

There was a particular photo
she loved, of Jeremy walking
down their garden – with his back to her,
through crisp, newly fallen snow.
Taken a year before he died,
she found it haunting, she said,
for its stillness – which somehow
transcended the certainty of his going.

If I were following strict chronology,
this photo would appear much earlier
in her story. But I place it here
because of what it taught me
about life's habit of foreshadowing,
foreshortening, foreknowing.

YEW

Foot tread, echo thread,
the hours move slowly
on pathway and porch way.

Dark hieroglyph,
inky tree, your long strokes
touch my window.

All day I read your shadow.
All night you translate me.

The Year's Midnight

in memory of Sally
d. 14 December 1999

I HOPE IN NOVEMBER

All coordinates were gone.
As the options narrowed down
on a familiar map, every inch of which
was named, and owned, and known,
nothing except what was beyond
the bounds of possibility would do.

Each found themselves
at the wordless edge, alone:
no stone unturned, no avenue
unexplored, no help unsought,
no territory uncharted.
Till finally, another scale came into view.

II HOURGLASS

I can remember the beginning
of this story, and how it ends.
The middle is slipping away,
into reticence.
Her room was like a bowl,
holding the hours tangible
and whole, like things
she had collected.
As she lay in bed,
watching the days
shortening,
clouds
passing,
shadows
moving,
wind
in the tree,
she drifted.
It wasn't silence
that came between us
but the eloquence
of what was left unsaid.
She wanted nothing more
than the sense of things continuing.

III ENLIVE

It's the brand name for a drink,
and it comes in three fruity flavours.
it has a pungent, sticky sort of smell.

The manufacturers pack it in cartons
for the terminally ill – small bright boxes,
just the right size for an average meal.

It contains all the nutrients
to keep a dying body
ticking over – tick tock tick.

    *

She had it as ice cubes and enjoyed it
for dessert. Towards the end, she took
to sucking it, like a lollipop on a stick.

And I've nothing against it, this essence,
this elixir, except its name: Enlive.
What blind fool came up with that?

An extra 'n' at the end would have been
encouraging, but the 'en' at the beginning
is completely crass, not to be forgiven.

    *

A curse on the committee
which nodded this name past,
making every breakfast

an uneasy transition,
making every lunch-time
a tactless reminder,

every supper her last.

IV HER WINDOW

was an eye staring out on the garden
and in on her last visitors
to-ing and fro-ing,

her blind a veined eyelid
opening closing, opening closing,
her sill a rim stained and silted,

her pane a lens where glazed light
beamed and glinted,
her room a cavity

where colours crept, gyrated.
Over the slack skin
of her bed, fringed shadows

lifted and shrank.
On her dark pupil
a tiny quartered window

dilated, deepened, sank
into a miniature inverted window
on a retina darker still.

V DECEMBER

Warm spine resting
against me now,

arms and shoulders
cradled by mine –

time stole up on you
like the tree's shadow.

VI THEN

the snow started to fall,
gently slowly softly –
a blanket of thick white snow –

sounds were muffled all around her
and a drifting motion
held her safe, cradled, peaceful, slow

as we watched her go
gently slowly softly
behind her counterpane of morphine.

She seemed to know that she'd been born
when it was snowing
and that she'd die in the snow.

VII (AND THEN AGAIN)

Of course that's not how it happened.
By the time I got there she was a long way
gone on morphine. And when she smiled
she can't have known that it was me.
(That afternoon, she'd been hallucinating:
we had arranged a party; she must get up,
get everything prepared.) And when she said
good-bye, I said 'I'll see you in the morning'.
And when I woke at three, it was the nurse,
not me, who watched beside her bed.
I wasn't there when she stopped breathing,
I was making tea. And when I saw her face
on the pillow – staring, yellow – it was dead.

VIII MORNING

Three hours, measured by
her missing heartbeat, between
the clink of milk bottles
on doorsteps and first light.

All night, snow has silently whitened
the houses. The treacherous streets
have hardened. In the shocked stillness,
every sound is magnified and sharpened.

She's gone. But outside in Moseley
the working day gets started. A door slams.
Someone shovels snow from their driveway.
A car's engine sputters, turns over, catches.

I open the door, and the cold rush of air
is a sudden intake of breath.
All's bright under a cloudless sky.
Light glints on crystal branches.

At the florists, they're setting out hyacinths,
holly and mistletoe, lilies and irises.
On the counter, black-eyed anemones glow
crimson and purple, like stained glass.

I pick my way back on the ice,
holding fresh tulips for her bedside.
Their tight pointed heads shine
clear as a torch against the blankness.

IX MEMBRANE

The tense has altered.

A wrong has been hushed up
by beauty, and sealed in by brightness.

I carry it with me through the morning
like an unsent letter or a secret debt.

By midday, the word is out,
the world is peopled by mourners.

Selves are composite,
bleed into each other.

From the outer surfaces of things
and from the edges of thoughts and feelings

a membrane has been softened
and quietly, violently, removed.

X UNTITLED

Your face
had changed
since I last saw you:
cheekbones higher
skin tighter
chin sharper
nose more aquiline
mouth more shrewd.
Skull on the pillow
skull on the pillow
when I kissed your forehead
I could swear your eyes moved.

XI TAKING STOCK

Ripping the remains
of a chicken into shreds,
putting the bones in a pan of water
and the nuggets of meat
carefully to one side

was useful: it taught us
the value of thrift, of husbandry –
the only metaphor I could find,
sorting through her belongings
a fortnight after she died.

XII THE HOUSE

Even now, as your life is packed in boxes,
it guards its secrets closely.
                                      That envelope
we just threw out contained the jottings
for an article. You wore this necklace
on the night of your wedding.
He learnt to crawl the day you took this photo.
You kept that because it was her best drawing.

When the removal vans start arriving
to cart your stuff away, the house will stand there,
silent as always, watching and listening.
Don't breathe a word: it won't change anything.

XIII HER SHOES

Put yourself in her shoes
I'll say every time I wear them.

They're backless, brown,
with sporty black soles

and a chunky purposeful look.
I'm told they're in fashion – funky.

I didn't steal them from her wardrobe
with the other gear after she died.

I tried them on beforehand.

*

How they suited me, how I loved them,
how I stomped about in them round her bed.

'They're great', I shouted.
'They're yours,' she said.

'Do I get them now?' I risked out loud.
'There's a limit,' she snapped –

and then, mock-pathetic, 'just give me
a chance to wear them first,' she begged.

(*I'd rather be in my shoes than yours*
I quipped, this time inside my head.)

*

We got by on this kind of repartee –
the bolder and blunter the better.

It was sisterhood, it was camaraderie,
and for a while we did it in style.

Now I have her shoes instead.

XIV KEEPSAKES

It must have been a month or so
before she died. I picture her propped
up in bed, with a tray of tea.

Emma brought her some drawings –
an abundance of them,
all variations on a single theme.

Together they sorted
and admired them,
selecting the best three:

a butterfly poised on a flower,
a girl with immense open hands,
and a beaming cat under a tree.

In exchange, she gave Emma a medallion
on a gold chain: 'pale blue, like your eyes,
to go down this side of the family.'

After the funeral,
we hid the necklace away.

Every so often we take it out,
and inspect it carefully: a tiny inlaid oval,
pale blue, like a cloudless summer sky.

At first we had a definite age
in mind, but as the years go by, no age
seems old enough, or special enough,

to wear it safely.

XV ANNIVERSARY

No snow came soundlessly
on this non day
from nowhere strangely

bringing muffled voices
and treacherous bouquets
draped in cellophane.

How you hated
(freesias the one exception)
these corpses fed on water and aspirin,

roses for visiting
lilies for burying
tulips for remembering:

a good show,
like the see-through coffin
you wore your best velvet in.

All the long morning
was your winding sheet unwinding
your body lifted from linen.

All afternoon
an immense bowl
of empty floodlit now

filling steadily with then
in slow motion
and then again.

XVI REMINDERS

Most are inevitable, like days
drawing in, or sun edging
round curtains each morning.

Others I can't predict, or explain –
like the way, at a corner of the High,
a flock of gulls rose suddenly

in rapid swirling rings, beating
their wings against the air, the light,
and crying your name, your name.

XVII ABOUT TIME

You were always so good
at being somewhere else.
Now you're there forever,

watching silently at my shoulder.
I would, if I could, tell you
how tall and brave a son he grew,

and never a day without comparing
the changing pattern of himself
to one you knew.

Ten years have passed, without you
even noticing. Be off with you.

Memory's Music

'This is the music of memory, water'
(Derek Walcott)

LAND'S END

Fathomless and free,
beyond the furthest edge of now and here,
where chartered land drops sudden, sheer,
to rough salt history,
the sea begins, the sea begins the mystery
of un-beginning sea.

Surging nearer, louder and more clear
through blank unmeasured waste of then and there,
sea-swell heaves, smashes,
scatters on the scree.

Crusted rock-pools pocket the spume's leavings:
stones worn silky thin,
an ammonite's rare coil,
      net, yarn, driftwood, a cork bob-bobbing,
fluted, involuted shell tubes,
feathers tipped with oil.

Sculpted and re-sculpted by the tide's harsh grain,
these frail things will vanish.

Their elements remain.

NAME-PLACING

A brawny arm reaches into the Atlantic –
all clenched thew, from gnarled elbow to bent knuckle –
clutching nothing between gigantic
forefinger and stubby thumb but buckle
of obdurate tide on gravel, lick
of wet salt in pocked groove and runnel.
Kehelland, Trethewey, Coverack, Castellack, pucker
its wrinkled skin like wens or carbuncles.
Mawnan, Mullion, Lamorna, Morvah
slither with Zennor like eels in channels,
or rise like furtive moles from under cover
of ridged veins and cropped stubble. Fluid, feral,
my own name, gripped between crag and ocean,
clings in its ancient rock-crease, a crustacean.

CHOUGHS

Lost heralds, outriders of a vanished
race. Beaky, black coated, melancholy;
eyes like hard drills that could bore
a hole from here to Land's End,
keen and cruel with intent.

Kyaa kyaa kyaa: a Celtic cry.
At night their trapped souls travel west, flap free
on the Cornish coastline, ride the rough wind sea-
ward, turn with the tide's turning, fly inland.

'What saw you there?' said the king.
'Sir', he said, 'I saw nothing
but the waters wap and the waves wan.'
Over Camelot the spirit soars
and slackens, spent.

PORTLOE: LOOKING WESTWARD

I love the broken
interrupted suddenness of it –
neither an absolute falling away,
nor a soft-contoured merging of land and sea,
but a stepping down
among angled planes and surfaces –
crenellated granite, an improvised structure
of jutting rooftops, chimneys, windows, balconies
(and hidden inlets, lost distances,
unseen promontories?)
to a harbour
scarcely wide enough for five fishing-boats,
a mound of crab-creels, rigging,
where the eye yields to sea's dissolving edge,
and waves move in the cove like a longing.

HIRAETH

Memory, you open
smoothly, like a great white shell
holding the ocean.

Your flanged auricle
funnels and cups the rushing
far-off sound of waves.

All your coiling twists
are clear, exact, retaining
long distant echoes.

Our ears touch. Listen –
the sea moves between us,
into hidden caves.

Even muffled sounds
come gradually closer:
amplified whispers.

'Listen', the waves say,
so we listen: 'Hiraeth'
they go on saying.

TERM-TIME

I toy with the sea-
urchins on my window-sill,
turning them over
and over, as if I could
recover their wet sea smell.

Cooped in college, where
the quad's four walls stare at each
other, I dream of
narrow roads tunnelling through
warm soft April mornings –

shadowy, primrose-banked,
going nowhere – with sudden
gaps of widening
light, and vistas of ocean:
hidden creeks, rocky inlets,

coves like hands cupping
impossible dreams of home,
where spring's benediction
is an everlasting
wash of sea, and hush of air . . .

The window's still open.
traffic noise drifts in. Even
with my eyes shut, I'm
neither here nor there, but
forever shuttling in between.

SECOND HOMES
in memory of Robert Woof

He told me, once, what it means to belong
to a place, why a place could never be a belonging.
'It's not home unless you've wintered there',
he said. I try to picture winters in Portloe:
nothing but pounding, pounding sea
and the remorseless circling cry of gulls.
Unending gunmetal grey of sky.
Fishermen cursing the weather. Up-ended hulls.
Year after year, one by one, the village houses
sold to weekenders, till all the local folk are gone.

And so my thoughts settle, come to rest on him
wintering in his cold home in Grasmere –
where cloud-shadows drift on the high fells
and wind blows free on Dunmail Raise or Silver How,
indifferent and conditional as the sea.

VERYAN GREEN

I remember it often: how the bells rang
all afternoon, the day we moved in –
Coleridge's 'sweet birthplace' running through
my mind, again and again, as the peals drifted
uphill to Veryan Green.

It's twelve years since we found the house;
three since it became our own.
We have friends in the village;
know some of the footpaths well.
I could find my way to Portloe
across the fields in darkness,
or describe in detail how the day's
shadows move slowly down the Row.

But still there are long intervals
in the almanac, marking each absence;
turns in each season I've never known.
The most I can say is that each year,
each day, I edge a bit further away
from the illusion that this is home.

THE ROAD TO VERYAN

Dappled banks fill
with cranesbill, ferns,
sorrel, brambles.

Weeds spurt and spill
over chill stones
and still crannies.

From weathered walls,
blackbirds call through
the tall grasses

down lanes stippled
with pink, tipsy
with triple blues:

Forget-me-not,
don't forget, not
yet forgotten.

*

In the playground
by the pond, all
year round, a stream's

murmuring sound –
and the wind lies
low under trees.

Children on swings
are laughing, where
swaying branches

half-screen the graves.
Nothing moves in
there, save the leaves –

but all day long
crickets sing their
rasping song, loud

among bending
grasses – thin and
thinning in the breeze.

*

Names of the dead
have faded on
mildewed marble.

Sea-gulls circle,
melancholy –
calling, crying

for the souls of
lost sailors, and
Hera's drowned crew

in their long ship-
shaped tomb, up here
on the steep hill.

Tall bracken waves
over graves mottled
and ivy-trailed:

grey-lichened stones
no one owns, where
old bones moulder.

At intervals,
the church bell sounds
its healing knell.

PENDOWER

My heart is tugged
by a silken thread
as I tread the path
by a silver stream
to the hollow way
in Pendower wood.

My eye is led
through the hollow way
between knotted banks
under arching trees
where branch-tips
touch and interlace
in Pendower wood.

My ear is tuned
to a single chord
by the sound of gulls
far overhead
as they wheel and call
from the tall green sides
of the rustling valley
in Pendower wood.

My thoughts are cradled
through the hollow way
by a rocking motion
of wind in the trees
and a dancing pattern
of light in the leaves
as I thread my way
with the silver stream
through Pendower wood.

My ear is tuned
to a swelling chord
my heart is held
by a lengthening thread
my thoughts are cradled
by the hollow way
as I follow the path
to a sheltered stretch
of scrubby ground
where a fringe of rushes
screens rock and sand
from Pendower Wood.

Wind slaps me hard
with a salty tang
as the screen of rushes
opens wide
where the tide comes in
with a rumbling sound
on the long yellow strand.
Gulls circle low
over rock and sea
as my eye is whelmed
by an empty, vast, cerulean sky.

WRACKS

I ROCK-POOLS AT CARNE

Rock-pools collect
old secrets, share
slow connections.

From pool to pool,
time moves, filling
them silently.

*

On this dark rock,
mussels, cockles,
barnacles have

all interlocked.
The pock-marked crust
is packed so thick

with limpets in criss-
crossing clusters
that its jagged

surface forms one
unbroken mat,
or skin. Under

a jutting ledge,
a dark edge of
sand ridges my

pond. Here a ring
of weed clings, its
cold fringe dripping.

*

Crenellated
overhead, the
pool-bed is deep

and still. It fills
and re-fills with
salt, chill water.

*

Worm-castings coil
in a pile on
the cold wet sand.

Their delicate,
intricate forms
await the tide.

II MERMAIDEN WEEDS

Their long green hair
fastens where wood
drifts,
        bare as bones,

or feathers float
in the slow ebb
and flow
        of ocean.

Combed to one side,
and matted by
the tide,
        they trail

bright wanton threads
on rock-beds, or
spread
        soft tresses

in crevices
which the sea's rude
tongue
        caresses.

III UNSOLVED RIDDLE

Your fronds quiver
        under water
like surreal hides.

You're not pie-bald
        but tri-bald. A
three-fold colour-

scheme has dappled
        your long sides in
marbled patterns

or striations –
        olive green, white,
dark brown. Often

I've seen you – mould-
        ering, old, draped on
paddled shorelines,

your ends splayed wide,
        ocean's pride, un-
identified.

IV FETCHED UP

Their blades are wedge-
    shaped, blunt-edged, with
pink-red leaflets
at the branch-tips.

            Tide-whipped, torn, they
                    fetch up in worn
                    pinky patches
            on beaches.
                        Sun
                    stretches them thin.

    Then the waves catch
        them, snatch them, and
    fetch them up again.

V REMEDIES

'Sea-weeds have the sea and all its medicinal properties in every cell.'

'Search in rock-pools for the healing simples
known as medicinal: minerals
are vital to life.' So goes the old wisdom:
told, re-told, sold, passed down.

Rachel Carson made it known, in her own
version: 'Earth depends on oxygen,
which Ocean provides. You, if you wish
for nourishment, must cherish it.'

Is it her I see, in my mind's eye,
as I search for specimens on the shore-line,
to take home and then examine,
in my own time turning them to rhyme?

VI TOOTHED WRACK

These licorice
    eels vanish when
        waves swish over –
      but like cladding
        their tough thongs grip
  and cling. Seething
in a single mass,
  the rock-face is
      black, glistening
    with nutrition:
  Earth's Ocean is
un-finishing.

VII BLADDER WRACK

Old bladder-wrack,
    dry and black,
           strewn
      on rock or sand.
The waves draw back,
      leaving
          slack strands
          to crack on land.

VIII OAR-WEED, OR TANGLE

Dismembered arms:
sodden, warm, flayed
thin,
        storm-scattered,

washed up in pools
on the sand,
            with
      limp hands flapping.

Their fingers fray,
            fade to grey – so
the sailors here say.

IX SEA-OAK

      Hold fast
    to your
   rock-face,
poor lone-
    some survivor.
     The sea's
       grim law
           keeps
      no score.
   Its old maw
tightens.

X OLD NAMES
Wireweed, Toothed Wrack, Channelled Wrack, Bladder Wrack, Knotweed, Grass Wrack...

Old names, clear as
loss, or Poor Man's
Weather-Glass –

Not used daily,
but sturdy and
made to last, like

the shipping forecast,
or a list of
choicest unguents.

Many of these
will always be
with us. Most will

pass. Names clear as
loss, the poor man's
weather-glass.

XI RE-CYCLED

Swallowed and spewed,
swallowed and spewed:

the sea preserves in old economy
what land steals back from memory.

HARVEST

Undulating lanes narrow, like furred arteries,
from May till late July – their tall sides
clogged with nettles, bracken, gleaming ivy,
and the long clambering arms of brambles.
Herringbone-patterned walls lose their edges –
moss-softened, swarming with purple foxgloves,
rusty sorrel, and ragged robin's delicate pink stars.
Clumps of valerian and clustering red campion
ramp in ruts or tug in cracks,
splashing rich pinks and scarlets.
Lush ferns throng the hedges – layer on layer
of fronds, all shades of emerald, citrine,
peridot, jade – so densely interwoven
you can scarcely tell where grassy bank
gives way to solid wall.

A caterpillar could lose its way in here,
mistaking the scant band of tarmac
for a sheep track. (A thought could peter out
in a thin aimless capillary,
wandering away from the main stem.)
A month longer, at this rate of growth,
and the shadowy lanes would be impassable:
the Roseland a maze of estranging ginnels,
each with a bright disc of endpoint light
dwindling day by day to a small dot,
almost imperceptible in the early morning drizzle.

And so, in August, the hedge-cutters come,
with their long strimmer blades – slicing
and carving, laying waste and clearing.
Verge, bank, wall, and beetling hedge stand sheer –
each lane a corridor, edged uniformly

with grey leafless thicket; each thicket sculpted
and planed; each branch, nest, twig, stalk
cut to the quick. You'd have to be made of stone
not to regret, not to look back.

Out in the open, more signs that Autumn
has come than that summer is still here:
the big beautiful fields of wheat and barley
which once swayed in the breeze like the sea
are stilled to stubble; and in the hay-fields
every golden cylindrical bale throws a long
sharp-edged shadow in the late August sun.

But the blackberries, darkly glistening
(with a month to go till the devil spits
on them) are plump, lush, warm, ready for
gathering – at least this side of the hedge.

HIGH TIDE IN OCTOBER

High tide is nearly over. Wavering lines
of sea-weed glisten in ridges all along the bay.
But still the ocean roars – pounding
the shoreline for hours
with immense white-foaming breakers,
chucking solid matter onto deserted beaches,
smashing on Nare Head in huge arcs of spray.

Carne beach is eerie as a moonscape,
or one of those cratered battlefields
painted by Paul Nash. Light glints
dimly through low mist on tussocks
and rocks draped with torn oar-weed.
Spars of wood jut out at all angles,
jagged against the gleaming strand.

Up on the high ground, yards
of sodden kelp, matted and swirled,
lie where the waves have flung them,
thick as fallen leaves or winter quilting:
all shades of crimson, copper, gold.
Summer's emerald rock-pools are gone,
turned to brown soupy puddles.

Lower down, close to the silver tideline,
wracks straggle in patches, loosely strewn,
their salty fronds tangled with multi-coloured
nylon yarn. Bubble-wrap, polythene bags,
sheets of cellophane, lie everywhere:
our indigestibles, thrown back at us
among the driftwood like useless toys.

'Ten years ago, these beaches were free
of plastic', says a man from Probus –
watching the waves come in, shaking
his head sadly: 'Now it's everywhere.'
As he speaks, his dog burrows excitedly
in a pile of black rubber piping
for something edible among the detritus.

Inches away from the curling waves,
crested blobs of dirty froth,
whipped stiff like egg-white,
shift slightly on the dark wet sand.
Iridescent bubbles, catching the light
like Christmas baubles, shine
the full spectrum of rainbow colours.

WALTER LANGLEY'S *THE BREADWINNERS*

The sea is tranquil now, at low tide
in the busy harbour. Boats are coming in
towards the lighthouse
as in a child's picture, their russet sails
pointing upward from a light blue
placid ocean into a pale grey sky.

Fishermen seen from a distance
unload their catch, while
off to the left (silhouetted like rocks
against the water) two women
forage for a pittance
among piles of seaweed.

All the elements of a maritime
working day are drawn together
to create a balanced composition,
so that the eye comes quietly to rest
on humdrum things
selected for what they signify:

in the middle ground a bottomless
basket, overturned where the sea
has left it, empty mouth agape;
in the bottom right-hand corner
damp bladder-wrack scrawled
over a stone like an artist's signature.

Yet how unflinchingly the three
old Newlyn fishwives are depicted
in their stoic trudge across the shining sand:
moving towards us, straining under
their burdens, filling the foreground
with their working bodies.

Here they come, in grubby threadbare aprons
and sand-caked shoes – baskets laden,
backs set stubbornly against the ocean:
two of them huddled together, as if joined
by hidden ties; the other walking apart,
her strong spirit all but broken.

Their faces are in shadow, but bowed
shoulders betray as much hardship
and endurance as lined foreheads
half-glimpsed under headscarves,
obdurate set of mouths and chins,
downward gaze of private, preoccupied eyes.

WRECK
after Barbara Hepworth

Keeled over, with half the rib-cage gone,
bones smoothed by water and wind:
is it a whale's carcass, stripped bare
by the gulls, or a boat's hull – stranded,
skeletal, visible only when the tide is low
and the estuary empties, leaving
alternating stripes of water and wet sand?

Perhaps neither of these things, exactly,
but a grammar of loss – a way of grasping
the shape and structure of desolation.
Examine it more closely, from all angles.
Is it a harp, or a cello? Listen. There are strings
on the struts for the wind to play its tunes on.
Feel the hewn, polished contours with your hand.

INVISIBLE

Behind you, whichever way you turn –
you'd know her again if you could see her:
hollow as the trunk of a great oak,
thick as three centuries;
deep as the wound where the branch tore
splitting the tree;
strange as this phantom limb
spreading new twigs – leaves stirring,
whispering, rippling like the sea;
gnarled as the riven wood waiting;
dark as the ribbed cavity where folds and folds
of lost time sink into absence.

REMEMBERING THE ECLIPSE
Written after a meeting with strangers at Dodman Point

           I

'No, we'll never forget,' she said,
'how the corridor of darkness,
dimly lit on either side,
moved steadily towards us.'

So a corridor of darkness,
from somewhere out of sight,
moved steadily towards
you in the hazy morning light?

'Yes, from somewhere out of sight
over there beyond the Lizard.'
It was in the hazy morning light
that they had travelled and gathered

from far around the Lizard.
'We climbed here, a crowd of us –
we travelled and gathered
to watch, like pilgrims, in silence.'

They'd climbed here, the crowd of them,
as if to witness a miracle,
and watched in silence like pilgrims
as the long cold shadow fell.

Had they witnessed a miracle?
Not a bird in sight up here
as the long cold shadow fell
and the dogs howled with fear.

'Not a bird in sight up here
on the cliff-edge in darkness,
and the dogs began to howl with fear
as we all stood in silence.'

Standing on the cliff in silence,
the sea on both sides brightly lit,
and all else in darkness:
'No', she said, 'We'll never forget it.'

II

I'll never forget that morning –
how we climbed as far as this;
how we met them and got talking
about that summer of the eclipse.

Had they climbed as far as this?
We questioned them minutely
about that summer and the eclipse,
thinking our own thoughts privately.

We questioned them minutely
about what had happened when,
thinking our own thoughts privately
as we went over it all once again.

Exactly what had happened then?
Was she already dying?
(They went over it all again.)
How could we have known it then?

She was already dying –
was the eclipse an augury?

No, we couldn't have known it then,
though I'd believed it, secretly.

Was the eclipse an augury?
As we met them and got talking
I believed so, secretly.
No, I'll never forget that morning.

A WINTER WALK
in memory of the crew of the Hera, *wrecked on Gull Rock, 1 February 1914*

Cold light slants
on gleaming roof-slates and thatches
where gulls call from chimney-stacks
over silent cottages.
The Roseland is powdered with frozen snow.
Glittering crystals cluster in a brittle coating
on moss-crammed walls
on stiles and gate-bars
on roads criss-crossed by shadows
on lanes pitted with crisp-topped puddles.
Inland, the fields are muted to grey-greens and ochres –
sheep, scattered thin on hillsides
still as stones.
Here on the cliff-path a territorial robin bobs
sudden and quick
among thick clumps of golden gorse,
head alert as a question.
Low sun pours wintry light on dazed blue depths,
glancing surfaces, incalculable distances.

At Nare Head we stop by a decoy centre
and a Cold War nuclear bunker,
fears of conflict driven deep into hiding
by melting light this February morning.
Even the haunted spot
where a hundred years ago the drowned crew
churned in dark waters
is calm – its shining membrane unruffled.
Gull Rock in silhouette is quiet as a mouse
nibbling a bit of cheese:

one ear upright against the quivering ocean,
body motionless, tail slack and thin.

My thoughts are slippery as grass
in sun-thaw – and oh, the sun is treacherous,
pouring its silver on the sea,
straight as a beam from Brittany,
into the tranquil wide-rimmed bay
where waves come in, over and over
and over again,
indifferent to human loss:
equalising, oblivious, clean.

ACKNOWLEDGEMENTS

This collection has been long in the making. I'd like to thank all the friends, colleagues and family members who have encouraged it to happen. In particular, I'm very grateful to have had attentive and generous feedback from Carmen Bugan, Sandie Byrne, Justin Gosling, Jane Griffiths, Peter King, and Wes Williams. Tom Clucas has been an insightful reader of the collection in its final form; and Stephen Stuart-Smith an ideal editor. It has also been a privilege to receive comments on some of the poems from fellow members of the Hall Writers' Forum.

The following poems (or earlier versions of them) have already been published elsewhere: 'Enlive' in the *Oxford Magazine*; 'Name-Placing' in *Poetry Cornwall*; 'French Windows', 'A Rebellion', 'Found' and 'The Swallows' in *Joining Music with Reason* (Way-wiser, 2008); 'Her face', 'Her shoes', 'Conkers' and 'From the loft: a dream of blue' in *Oxford Poetry*; 'Your Lost Poem' and 'Anniversary' in the *Oxford Poets Anthology* (Carcanet, 2004); 'Choughs' in *Chatter of Choughs: The Return of Cornwall's Legendary Bird*, ed. Lucy Newlyn (Hypatia: Penzance, 2006); and 'Stray' in *Branch-Lines: Edward Thomas and Contemporary Poetry*, ed. Guy Cuthbertson and Lucy Newlyn (Enitharmon Press, 2007).